**To Catch an Elephant**

**Previous publications by Gerard Benson**
*Name Game* (Oyster Publications 1971)
*Gorgon* (a poem in eight parts) (Paranomasia Press 1984)
*The Magnificent Callisto* (Blackie Poetry Originals 1992/
   Puffin 1993)
*In Wordsworth's Chair* (Flambard Press, in association
   with the Wordsworth Trust, 1995)
*Evidence of Elephants* (Viking 1995) (nominated for the
   Carnegie Medal 1996)
*Bradford & Beyond* (Flambard Press 1997)
*Hlep!* (fifteen poems with woodcuts by Ros Cuthbert)
   (Yellow Fox Press 2001)

Co-editor: *Poems on the Underground* Anthologies (ten
   editions); *Love Poems on the Underground; London
   Poems on the Underground; Funny Poems on the
   Underground*
Editor: This *Poem Doesn't Rhyme* (Viking 1990/Puffin
   1992) (winner of the Signal Poetry Award 1991); *Does
   W Trouble You?* (Viking 1994/Puffin 1995)

Some of the poems in this book have been published in
*Strolling Players, The New Oxford Book of Children's Verse,
Hello New!, 'Ere We Go, Unzip Your Lips, Loopy Limericks,
The New Puffin Book of Funny Verse, The Love of Cats,
Otherworlds, Swings and Shadows, The Oxford Book of
Animal Poems, The New Oxford Treasury of Children's
Poems, Headlines from the Jungle*.

# To Catch an Elephant

Poems by Gerard Benson

Illustrated by Cathy Benson

*Smith/Doorstop Books*

Published 2002 by
Smith/Doorstop Books
The Poetry Business
The Studio
Byram Arcade
Westgate
Huddersfield HD1 1ND

ISBN 1-902382-40-4

A CIP catalogue record for this book is available from the British
Library.

Typeset at The Poetry Business
Printed by Charlesworth & Co. Ltd., Huddersfield
Cover design by Cathy Benson

Distributed by Central Books Ltd., 99 Wallis Road, London E9 5LN

The Poetry Business gratefully acknowledges the help of Kirklees
Metropolitan Council and Yorkshire Arts.

# CONTENTS

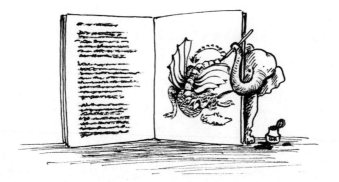

*For my big brother, Julian, and my little brother, Nicolas*
GB


*For Sue, Ien and Fraser, with love*
CB

**Gerard Benson** was born and brought up in London. He was evacuated for a while during the Second World War – so he came to enjoy the country as well as the big city.

He has written poetry since he was a child but has earned his living in many ways. He has been a sailor, labourer, window-cleaner, waiter, washer-up, market researcher, actor, architect's clerk, teacher, postman, temp. and lecturer, among other things – and of course a poet and editor.

With two friends he runs the 'Poems on the Underground' scheme in London. For many years he toured, performing poetry and music with the famous Barrow Poets.

His son and daughter are now grown up. He lives in Yorkshire with his illustrator wife, Cathy.

**Cathy Benson** was born in Bradford but she spent her childhood in a seaside town in Scotland.

She always drew. No writing pad, envelope or paper bag was safe from her, and when she ran out of paper she drew in the sand.

When she grew up she married, had three children, became a teacher, owned five cats, reared stray animals: woodmice, assorted birds, hedgehogs, beetles (yes! beetles), frogs, crayfish and even a duck.

She left teaching to do more writing and painting and to travel with her second husband, the poet Gerard Benson.

Her mind has travelled through the poems in this book and these are the pictures she saw.

## To Catch an Elephant

Requires patience and attention to detail
But any girl or boy should be able
To master this method; it's quite simple.
Physical strength is not necessary
Nor is specialized knowledge;
But you will require quick thinking, courage,
A few simple skills – and of course luck.
(If you are not a lucky person
Do not even consider it, but purchase
Your elephant from a reputable dealer.)

You will need: some buns, a step-ladder,
Binoculars, blackboard and chalk, tweezers,
A match box,* and (unless you are already there)
A ticket to India or Africa.
Use can also be found for a small table
Not to mention a good barrier cream and a sun hat.

> \* Note: For African elephants you should use
> the larger 'kitchen-size' match box.

Right! Display the buns on the table.
On the blackboard write in large letters:
FREE BUNS!    JUMBO OFFER!
Having done so, climb up the ladder
(Which should be placed in the cover
Of a bombax tree) and wait.
The binoculars may be used to scan the horizon
(Which is usually to be found some distance away,
Where the sky and the earth meet).
Elephants will eventually emanate.
Keep very still. This is the crucial moment.
The herd will approach, attracted by your notice.

While they are choosing their buns
You should be choosing your elephant
(Plump for one with a nice flexible trunk
And well-spaced ears). Now, when your elephant
Is picking up its bun (you could use cup cakes)
It will be momentarily distracted.
This is the time for action.
With a practised flick of the wrist,
Quickly reverse the binoculars
And look through them at your selected elephant.
Grasp it firmly with the tweezers,
Lift gently and place in the match box
(Which should have been lined with cotton wool).

## A Small Star

*I* live on a small star
Which it's my job to look after;
It whirls through space
Wrapped in a cloak of water.

It is a wonderful star:
Wherever you look there's life,
Though it's held at either end
In a white fist of ice.

There are creatures that move
Through air, sea and earth,
And growing things everywhere
Make beauty from dirt.

Everything is alive!
Even the stones:
Dazzling crystals grow
Deep under the ground.

And all the things belong,
Each one to the other.
I live on a precious star
Which it's my job to look after.

## *Moon Music*

*T*he Man in the Moon plays a tune
On a very old Silver Bassoon,
With a Thousand Guitars and a Chorus of Stars;
And they sail in a Giant Balloon
(Balloon)
They sail in a Giant Balloon.

And the Music they make is so fine
It tickles and tingles your spine.
As they play up on high, they light up the sky.
They sing as they play as they shine
(They shine)
They sing as they play as they shine.

And children tucked up in their beds
Hear that lovely old tune as it spreads
And the heavenly themes give them beautiful dreams,
While the music sings on in their heads
(Their heads)
The music plays on in their heads.

With a Thousand Guitars on the tune,
And a wonderful Silver Bassoon
The Music so grand fills the sea and the land
When it's played by the Man in the Moon
(The moon)
When it's played every night on the Moon.

## A Tale of Two Citizens

I have a Russian friend who lives in Minsk
And wears a lofty hat of beaver skinsk,
(Which does not suit a man so tall and thinsk).
He has a frizzly beard upon his chinsk.
He keeps his britches up with safety pinsk.
    'They're so much better than those thingsk
    Called belts and brackeies, don't you thinksk?'
    You'll hear him say, the man from Minsk.

He has a Polish pal who's from Gdansk,
Who lives by selling drinksks to football fansk,
And cheese rolls, from a little caravansk.
(He finds it pleasanter than robbing banksk).
He also uses pinsk to hold his pantsk.
    'Keep up one's pantsk with rubber bandsk!?
    It can't be donesk! It simply can'tsk!
    Not in Gdansk!' he'll say. 'No thanksk!'

They're so alikesk that strangers often thinksk
That they are brothers, yesk, or even twinsk.
'I live in Minsk but I was born in Omsk,'
Says one. His friend replies, 'That's where *I'm* fromsk!
Perhapsk we're brothers after all, not friendsk.'
    So they wrote homesk and asked their Mumsk
    But found they weren'tsk; so they shook handsk
    And left for Minsk, and for Gdansk.

## Oleg Popov the Clown

*I* saw him standing on a slackwire
Juggling with rings –
Standing on one foot on a slackwire
Juggling. Rings spun through the air
In profusion
To be caught,
So many! so many
Rings.
And he tossed and caught them
With such clownish ease.

Then the wire began to sway
To the left
To the right
Too far. Too far! Too FAR to the left
Too too far to the right.
'He's going to fall!' I thought
'He's going to fall!'

The crowd held its breath.

Twenty thousand breaths were held in.

And he fell! –
Less than half a metre.

And as he landed
Wallop! on his bum
He raised his hands

Also his feet
And caught those rings
As one by one they dropped.

Before he would climb again onto the uncertain slackwire
He took a handful of straw from his pocket,
And placed it on the ground
Under the wire
To cushion his landing
In case he should again
Fall, while the rings
Were flying through the air.

## River Song

'*O*h where are you going?' said Rover to river,
'You flow always downward. Why should that be?'
'I gather the droplets of water together
And carry them home to their mother, the sea.'

'From moment to moment,' said Rover to river,
'Your waters are changing, yet you stay the same.'
'No. I am the mocker of every map-maker;
Although they outline me and give me a name.'

'I'm banked and I'm bridged,' said river to Rover.
'I'm built by; I'm fished in, I'm wished on as well.
But I am a winder; I love to wander.
Every day I am different, with stories to tell,'

'Of floods and disasters,' said river to Rover,
'Of long lazy summers, of ducks in my weeds,
Of wild otter huntings, of strange ghostly hauntings,
Of crisp frozen winters with ice on my reeds.'

'Of towns that surround me,' said river to Rover,
'Until I escape through the bridges, to fields
Where brown cattle wallow beside my green willows,
And small beetles strut, with their bright shining shields.'

'And all the time downward,' said river to Rover,
'I travel past building and boulder and tree.
I gather the driplets and droplets together
And hurry them home to their mother, the sea.'

## Wasp

*A* slim city slicker, sharp
In his black and yellow outfit,
He fines to a point of venom;
Winged singer, ruthless marauder
Whose soft head radiates fear.
God's pleasure in his workmanship
Is nowhere clearer to be seen
Than in this sleek visitor
To picnic and summer kitchen –
Perfect, beautiful and deadly.

Crawling on glass he is clumsy, a fumbler;
His mastery is shown in the air,
Riding without effort, landing on a jam pot.
He can patrol a straight line
Inches above the floor.

## The Paper Beetle

*L*ook. There's a beetle
Lying where it's fallen,
By the foot of the bed;
An origami beetle
Cleverly made
Of birthday wrapping paper:
Head, thorax
And six, angular legs.

It's so still you might suppose it dead;
But listen to the song inside its head.

I'm …
A …
Paper beetle a paper beetle.
I scuttle onward, for ever onward,
I hurry forward, over grasses,
I'm up a seedling and down another.
I'm always moving. I'm never stopping,
Across the grass which is splashed with sunlight
And barred with shadow. I dodge the spider.
I just keep crawling with all my legs and I
Scuttle on and I scuttle on.

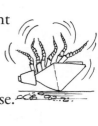

Through leaves and petals, until I fall, of course.
If I fall I shall wave my legs until,
Wave my legs until, wave my legs until,
Wave my legs until, wave my legs until
Something happens and I'll scurry on,
Then I'll hurry on. Then I'll hurry on …

## The Scholar's Cat

*P*angur, my white cat, and I,
We each a different skill apply;
His art is all in hunting mice,
Mine is in thought, deep and precise.

My greatest joy is just to sit
And con my page with subtle wit;
While Pangur Ban will frisk and play
Nor envy me my quieter way.

We are companions, never bored
In our small house, in true accord
We test our faculties, and find
Some occupation for the mind.

He, by his arts, can trap and kill
A hapless mouse with perfect skill.
And I, after much careful gleaning
Can bring to light a hidden meaning.

His eye, as keen as any sword,
Is focused on the skirting board;
While I direct my milder looks
Upon the knowledge in my books.

When he pursues a mouse with speed,
Pangur rejoices in the deed;
I exult when in the brain
Some knotty point at last comes plain.

Though we are always thus together,
We neither one obstruct the other;
Pangur and I pursue alone
Two separate arts, to each his own.

His curious work is his delight,
Which he rehearses day and night;
And daily I bring clarity
Where there had been obscurity.

*Note: This is a translation of a ninth-century Irish poem,
the first ever to mention the domestic cat.*

## The White Mouse

my
  eye
is a wink!
  a whisk
  my
    frisk-
          y
          tail;
    my
         pink
feet
      spread
under
      my
few
  ounces
i
      sit
  upright
       and hold
my feed
          be
            tween

my

        fingers.

my drink

  i nuzzle.

inqu-

     is-it (?)

        ive

i am

  and twitchy.

i sleep

    and wake

to my

    own

  small rhythms.

i stare

     blink

and am


    gone.


Twink!

## The Dragon and the Author

*T*he writer's pen moved and the dragon, all
But tamed, waddled his innocuous way
Through the dull pages of an empty tale
Beaming at kids and giving rides, while they
Well-washed and pretty, waved from his ridged back,
Prised fingers in between his tender scales;

But sometimes you might capture just a look,
Rapt, secret, in the eyes of a boy or girl
Who rode, as though the ancient furnace smouldered still
Beneath their bodies. If this was so, none spoke.
But some were found who strangely danced one day
And while they danced, the rumbling dragon's smoke
Rose high above the ruined citadel
Spelling old runes across the silent sky.

And when the writer started Chapter Twelve
And slowly spelled the dragon's secret name
The paper swiftly crackled into flame
And from the flame there rose an acrid smell.
Devouring teeth clashed on the moving quill
A cavernous mouth engulfed the writer whole
And drew him down into the reeking bowel.

## *The Dragon Speaks*

*I* knew I was the last of the line
That the continuance of dragonkind
Depended on me but thought I was safe.

We were (or rather, I was)
A protected species,
And since I was extremely pregnant
(expecting a clutch within the century)
I was escorted everywhere
By the RSPCMB*

That doomed day I was being exercised
In the Mythical Beings' Sanctuary
By a nice but gormless girl volunteer
When out of nowhere it seemed
Galloped this psychopath,
A butcher called George
Disguised in the insignia
Of the International Red Cross
But dressed underneath to kill
In an iron suit.

He thundered straight at me,
Lance to the fore.

I'd no time to dodge. (Well, I wasn't expecting
anything)
And my wings were clipped so I couldn't fly
(Besides there was no room for take-off).
I spat a little fire
But only singed his horse.

Then he hit me,
Clean between the ventral plates.
Then pain.
Then planets in a dance.
Then darkness.

The rest is mythology.

*Royal Society for the Prevention of Cruelty
to Mythical Beings*

## Three Birds

*T*hree birds flew in a clouded sky.
One was you and one was I
      And no-one knows the other.

The sky was heavy, soft and warm,
And off we flew to cheat the storm,
      You, I and the other.

To cheat the storm, away we flew;
One was white and one was blue.
      A raven was the other.

We flew to far-off countries, where
Soft waters speak to brittle air,
      Always with the other.

And there we bathed in silver springs
And shook the water from our wings;
      And with us came the other.

And in those fair, enchanted lands,
We built our nest upon the sands;
      And still with us the other.

And when we sang, the trilling notes
Like liquid, rippled from our throats;
     He never sang, that other.

Three birds mount toward the sun;
One is you, and I am one
     And no-one knows the other.

## The Cat and the Pig

*O*nce, when I wasn't very big
I made a song about a pig
    Who ate a fig
    And wore a wig
And nimbly danced the Irish jig.

And when I was as small as THAT
I made a verse about a cat
    Who ate a rat
    And wore a hat
And sat (you've guessed) upon the mat.

  And that, I thought, was that.

But yesterday upon my door
I heard a knock; I looked and saw
    A hatted cat
    A wiggèd pig
    Who chewed a rat
    Who danced the jig
    On my door mat!

They looked at me with faces wise
Out of their bright enquiring eyes,
'May we come in? For we are yours,
Pray do not leave us out of doors.
We are the children of your mind
Let us come in. Be kind. Be kind.'

So now upon my fireside mat
There lies a tireless pussy cat
Who all day long chews on a rat
    And wears a hat.
And round him like a whirligig
Dancing a frantic Irish jig
Munching a fig, cavorts a big
    Wig-headed pig.

They eat my cakes and drink my tea.
There's hardly anything for me!
And yet I cannot throw them out
For they are mine without a doubt.

But when I'm at my desk tonight
I'll be more careful what I write.

## The Aquarium

In a swift glint,
  In a wriggle of silver,
The dentist's fish
  Visits the stony
Bottom of the tank;
  Gobbles a small stone
And spits it back,

Bubbles lift
  Themselves through leaves.
A goldfish, hidden
  In a plastic palace
Twitches fin and tail
  And gracefully swishes
Into the weeds.

And the young boy
  Watches and watches.
He forgets his pain
  Just for a minute.
He gazes enthralled
  At this slow fish-dance
Till his name is called.

## Ant Number 1,049,652

Like a small yacht over a sea of grass
He tacks, carrying a green sail of leaf.

On the goad of his own acid he hastes
To receive or bestow a merciless death.

War machine directed by an unseen commander,
Minute mobile bottle of lethal chemical.

His mind lies outside his body. He is a fury
Of unbending purpose. The leaf will be delivered.

*Evidence of Elephants*

*If* you had had just the bones to go on,
  Only the bones,
Could you have guessed an elephant?
  How could you know?

Oh, you could work out the size and so on
  By measuring the bones,
But the vast flapping ears, that caked-mud grey,
  They would not show.

Nor the trunk. From the skull you'd never guess
  At that long swinging trunk,
Boneless and flexible, sensitive and beautiful,
  Hanging in front,

Or lifted to blare like a trumpet, or to caress
  Another elephant.
If I had only the bones to help me
  I think I'd be stumped.

## Bei-shung

*I* am *Bei-shung,* they call me the white bear.
I am the hidden king of these bamboo forests,
Invisible with my white fur and my black fur
Among this snow, these dark rocks and shadows.

I am the hidden king of these mountain heights,
Not a clown, not a toy. I do not care
To be seen. I walk, for all my weight,
Like a ghost on the soles of my black feet.

Invisible with my black fur and my white fur
I haunt the streams. I flip out little fishes;
I scoop them out of the water with my hand.
(I have a thumb, like you. I have a hand.)

Among this sparkling snow, these rocks and shadows,
I roam. Time is my own. My teeth are massive.
My jaw is a powerful grinder. I feed
On chewy bamboo, on small creatures, fish, birds.

You call me Panda. I am King *Bei-shung.*

## The Cloth Bird

The cloth bird hangs by the window
  On a length of string,
And all the birds in the garden
  Visit her and sing.

She hangs quite still in the window,
  Motionless for hours –
A warbler of white linen,
  Covered with blue flowers.

Then a breath of wind will move her,
  Rock her here and there –
But all the birds in garden
  Are free as the air.

The cloth bird is silent.
  She has no tongue.
But all the birds in the garden
  Fill the air with song.

They load the air with music:
  Twittering, cheeping, trilling,
Pink-a-pink, Cheeve-a-chee –
  Music so thrilling.

The cloth bird listens
  While the garden birds sing –
Hanging by the window
  On a piece of string.

## Duffy

The white cat furies
In a squirm of purring.

He writhes in his delight,
Rolling his restless head
He tunnels my ready lap.

He loops his length
Hooping his lithe spine.

The white cat settles,
Licks at a stiffened leg,
Then sleeps – a lazy shape.

The white cat dreams of snow fields,
The small musical pipes of birds,
Licking his lips in sleep.

# *Fishing*

*T*here is a fine
line

between fishing
and standing
on the bank
like
an idiot.

## Spot the Difference

The two pictures look very much alike.
In both a boy is diving into a swimming pool.
A girl sits, dangling her feet in the water.
A nice woman in a flowery frock
Is pointing at something we cannot see.
And a faithful dog I have nicknamed 'Soldier'
Is standing guard over a tennis ball.
There is a table laid for a picnic tea.

I am spotting the differences. There should be ten.
Look. There's no logo on the second boy's trunks,
And the second girl has only one hair ribbon.
And mummy number two – her watch has gone.
I don't like it. The bird has flown from the sky,

There's an extra cloud on the horizon,
And the swimming pool ladder has lost some rungs.
(That's six.) Oh, and Soldier has only one eye.

Who has done this to these nice people?
Look. They've got no milk for their tea;
Their jug has disappeared. Somebody hates them –
There are only three legs to their picnic table.
Which leaves me with just one to get.
(And to think I thought both pictures the same!)
Got it! Where mummy is pointing – there in the
        shrubbery –
Among those badly drawn leaves, isn't that

The muzzle of a rifle? And who is it pointing at?

## Goal!

It's Dicky to Dirty,
And Dirty back to Dicky ...
He swerves past three men
        (Oh, he's tricky)
And he lofts the ball
Into the middle,
A pin-point pass,
        Which finds Diddle;
Diddle back-heels
(Very neat, that, clever!)
And lays it in the path
        Of Trevor,
Our six million pound
Striker (well 25p
If you want the truth)
        And he
Drives it, right-footed;
It strikes the bar
And rebounds into the path
        Of Pa
(Our oldest player)
But unluckily it hits
His walking stick ...
        He sits
Suddenly, and the ball
Trickles back to Trevor,
Who shoots!! Unstoppable!!!
Did you ever!?!?

Their goalie palms
It away but straight
To Dozy (who's asleep) …
        But wait …!
Patch has got the ball
(He's half collie –
Recently signed from Rovers)
        And, golly!
He's nose down, tail up–
He's running rings
Round a sheepish defence –
        He brings
The leather to the educated feet
Of Gerard* (You bet!)
Now one neat flick and it's
        In the Net!

*Note: Or, if you like, put in your own name
and come off the bench as a late substitute.

*Sir Bert*

*T*here once was a knight, called Sir Bert
Who said; 'Oh, this armour *does* hurt!
　　I can stand it no more;
　　Nip down to the store
And fetch me a non-iron shirt.'

*Hlep!*

Something has gone wrog in the garden.
There are doffadils blooming in the nose-beds,
And all over the griss dandeloons
Wave their ridigulous powdered wigs.

Under the wipping willop, in the pond
Where the whiter-lollies flute,
I see goldfinches swamming
And the toepaddles changing into fargs.

The griss itself is an unusual shade of groon
And the gote has come loose from its honges.
It's all extrepely worlying!
Helg me, some baddy! Heap me!

And it's not unly in the ganden.
These trumbles have fellowed me indares.
The toble has grown an extra log
And the Tally won't get Baby-See-Too.

Even my trusty Tygerwriter
Is producing the most peaqueueliar worms.
Helg me Sam Biddy. Kelp me!
Helg! HOLP! HELLO!!

## The Inventor's Advertisement

Professor de Brayno, Inventor-at-Large
Will invent what you need at a very small charge.
Just give me a ring or a personal call;
No job is too large – and no job is too small.

To show you my skill at this neatest of crafts,
I've invented a cat-flap that keeps out all draughts
(Though it does admit chessmen, I'm working on that,
And I still haven't solved one last problem – the cat
Refuses to use it!) However, it looks
Very splendid indeed! I've a telly that cooks,
With a channel for beans and another for jelly
(Which is more than you get with your average telly).
I've a one-leggèd table, a two-leggèd stool
And a marvellous three-leggèd desk for your school.
I've invented a shirt with retractable sleeves
And a burglar alarm that can recognize thieves,
And odourless trainers, and non-falling socks,
And self-winding ear-rings (they're 10p a box).
I've a bicycle wheel with invisible spokes,
A Gigglecomputer that makes up new jokes,
A silent alarm clock that saves you from waking
And some edible glue that stops jelly from shaking.

I've inventions for this and inventions for that,
So if you're in need, and would like a brief chat,
Just pick up your phone now and give me a ring;
My number is … dash it! … oh bother the thing!
I've forgotten my number! I know what we'll do!
If you need some Inventing, why *I will ring you!!*

## A Magic Tent

Inside this tent
The world is different.
Balls thrown in the air
Stay there;
They spin from hand to hand
And never land.

The lovely lady in sparkling tights
Flies like a bird between the lights,
Now gold, now twinkling blue,
Now red, now every rainbow hue.
Before our very eyes
She changes colour as she flies.

High on a wire a fat man dances
And way below a pony prances,
Carrying a girl with a spangly shirt
And floating ballet skirt,
Who stands up proud
On one foot, blowing kisses to the crowd.
It's impossible! It's magical!!

Only the clowns tumble and fall.
With their strange noses and their enormous shoes,
They trip; then rise again: they never really lose.
While drums kerthump and trumpets flare and blare,
We stare, just stare.
Amazement!

And if they whisked the top off this fantastic tent,
Would everything be quite the same
As when we came?
Would we
Look up and see
The sky, that old familiar blue?
Or something new?
A Universe new-made, where dogs and cats
And Aunts and Uncles swing like acrobats,
With girls and boys, and even their Mas and Pas,
On heavenly trapezes, slung from the moon and stars?*!***

## Trombone Man

*(for Kid)*

*He* played upon the sad trombone,
The sad trombone, the sad trombone.
A minor tune of tender tone
He played upon the sad trombone,
From which a purple flower grew
Whenever he blew, whenever he blew;
And streams of bulging bubbles, too,
Which floated far above the town
And never burst, nor wandered down;
Or melting chocolate would pour
Its sweetness on the dancing floor,
Where rocking stompers swung and grooved,
And rhythmed as the music moved.

And while he played the sad trombone,
And slid the slider in and out,
I thought I heard a dancer shout:
'Oh look, how back and forth he slides
That slider; see the way it glides
Under the lights, so golden yellow,
And hear the music, dark and mellow
That billows from the sad trombone.'

And then the prooping sousaphone
Began; the wriggling clarionet,
The drumskin and the bright trum-pet,
Slap-happy bass and tall pi-anner,
All joined the song in stately manner,
Adding a sweep of harmony
To that unrolling melody.

Each line of music, soft or loud,
Spoke sadness to that dancing crowd,
But most of all, the wailful moan
Of him who blew the sad trombone,
His head thrown back, his cheeks outblown,
The eyes of one who thinks alone,
His thumping two-tone shoes emphatic,
His stance, his pumping arm dramatic,
As with his breath he coaxed along
Through puckered lips that minor song,
Upon that sad, that sad trombone!
That glad trombone, that mad trombone.
The sad trombone, the sad trombone,
The sad, the mad, the glad
Trom-
      bone.
          Yeah.

# Postcards in 23 Words

## Postcard from Fairyland

Spell-binding scenery.
Lots of moonbathing,
(no tan).
Food delicious,
portions small.
Elves quarrelsome.
Was granted three wishes –
messed it up.
So home Thursday.

## Postcard from Anywhere

I lie in bed
quite without fear,
play in the sand,
swim by the pier.
Having a wonderful time.
Glad you're not here.

## Postcard from Three-Bear Cottage

Not much of a holiday.
The furniture is broken.
Daddy Bear booms all the time –
Baby Bear squeaks.
Nothing to eat but porridge.

## Postcard from the North Pole

Surrounded by icy whiteness.
It's winter, and it's always night.
The stars twinkle forever.
But I miss you all –
and home –
and sunlight.

SNOWTEL

*Spring Assembly*

*R*ight! As you all know,
It's spring pretty soon
And I want a real good one this year.
I want no slackers. I want SPRING!
That's S-P-R-I-N-G! Got it?
Spring! Jump! Leap!
Energy! Busting out all over!
Nothing so beautiful! Ding-a-ding-a-ding!

Flowers: I want a grand show from you –
Lots of colour, lots of loveliness.
Daffodils: blow those gold trumpets.
Crocuses: poke up all over the parks and gardens,
Yellows, purples, whites; paint that picture.
And a nice show of blossom on the fruit trees.
Make it look like snow, just for a laugh,
Or loads of pink candy floss.

Winds: blow things about a bit.
North, South, East, West, get it all stirred up.
Get March nice and airy and exciting.

Rain: lots of shimmering showers please.
Soak the earth after its winter rest.
Water those seeds and seedlings.

And seeds: start pushing up.
Up! Up! Up! Let's see plenty of green.

Sunshine! give the earth a sparkle
After the rain. Warm things up.

And you birds: I haven't forgotten you.
Fill the gardens with song.
Build your nests (you'll remember how).
And you lambs: set an example,
Jump, leap, bound, bounce, spring!

And kids: ditch those coats and scarves,
And get running and skipping.
Use that playground, none of this
Hanging about by the school wall
With your hands in your jeans pockets.
It's spring, I tell you.
And you're part of it
And we've got to have a real good one this year.

## Whispers in the Wood

*D*id you see me when you came into the wood?
Did you not? You didn't see me at all?
I wasn't hiding. I was watching for you.
Did you notice the colour of the dry stone wall
Shift from goose-grey to buttery? Didn't you at all?

You say it often does that. Yes. And I'm usually there.
But perhaps, instead, you heard me? Surely you
     heard?
Nothing? You heard nothing? The wood went
     suddenly silent?
That was me. The trill of an unknown bird
Through the copse? It could have been me you heard.

Did you notice a spider web that billowed like a sail?
Were you not visited by an unexpected thought
About someone who may have lived in this wood
At some time in the past? Were you caught
Unawares? Were you sad? … I was that thought.

I have been watching for you, and waiting.
You like this wood. So do I. I know you well.
You do not see me but I'm not far away.
When you come here to play, do you not catch a smell
Sometimes in autumn? Do you never sense my
     presence? Well …?

## The Tree Nymph

*I* have forgotten now what my sin
   May have been,
Or how I enraged the old gods
   Of these woods.

But I remember how my feet
Began to grow long roots
And burrowed deep into the ground;
And how my arms and hands
Changed where I stood, bending
And flexing and slowly ascending,
Till they sprouted green leaves,
And stood high in the air and waved,
With all the winds that blow;
And how my body bent like an archer's bow
Into this shape that you see now.
If you look at my bark in the right place
You may see my gnarly face.

Touch my skin, my bark
   As you pass by.
Put your ear to my trunk.
   Do you hear a cry?

## Time is Eating the Cliffs

Time is eating the cliffs,
Slowly digesting them.

Come snow, come rain,
High tide and low,

Grain after grain,
Come breeze, come gale,

Come ice, come sun,
Time is eating the cliffs.

For a small while
Time will allow

Grasses to grow
In cracks of the cliffs,

Flowers to show
Their bright brave faces,

And will slyly reveal
The ancient hieroglyphs,

The curves and spirals,
The tough, ridged braille

Of ammonites, belemnites
Entombed aeons ago –

Fossil remains
To remind you of this:

That day by day,
Bite by tiny bite,

Time, who made the cliffs,
Is eating them away.

## To Time

*S*hadows on the grass,
And last year's oak leaf.
The minutes pass.
Shadows on the grass.
That sun-dial, that hour-glass;
Don't touch them, you thief!
Shadows on the grass.
Last year's oak leaf.

## *Poem for the Changing of the Clocks*

This hour
   in the night
      When I wait
         in the dark
            bedroom
               for sleep to take me away
     Passes with tick
       and tock
         of the wooden clock,
And I hear also
   in my imagination
      The silent breathing
         in    out
           in    out
Of a thousand other
  listeners to the night.
Cats stalk the slates
On firm and soundless feet
And tear the darkness with their yowls.
The joists and timbers
  stretch and sigh,
Ghosts in the attic creak.
  And dew beads the listening sycamore
That inks the space
  between me and the indifferent moon.

And this is the hour, perhaps
That will never be,
That will be looped into time
As the clocks of England
Adjust after their long summer
   To the rigours of Greenwich.

A child turns in its sleep
and somewhere an aged tap
   drips
        and
             drips.

## The Magnificent Callisto

Callisto cuts the cards
Using a sharp blade;
Doves fly out of his eyes.

A lady in glittering tights
Vanishes; in her place
Multitudinous stars

Play waltzes on little flutes.
Callisto conjures the King of Spades,
The swagged curtain stirs.

Now the show can truly commence!

There is a ball that hovers in the air;
There are pink fish that swim through glass;
There are artificial falls, that drop

Making trickles of tiny diamonds
On Callisto's assistant's cheeks.
Listen to the applause!

Now watch as the parts
Of the sawn-in-half man
Dance on the stage's boards,

Through which, predictably, spring
Flowers, spring flowers.
And then the curtain falls.
And then the curtain calls.

## The Injection

*I* lined up near the door
Just behind Maggy Moore.
We'd rolled up our sleeves,
And I could see her arm,
All freckly, like Steve's,
And rather thin. *No harm*
*In asking,* I thought.
So I said, 'Are you scared?'
'A bit,' she said. 'Are you?'
'No,' I said. But I'd been taught
Not to lie, so I said,
'Well, that's not really true.
I am, a bit, too.'

I stood with my arm bared,
And thoughts whizzing round in my head.
One at a time we went in.
'Last of this batch,'
Said the nurse. She rubbed my skin
With something cold. Then, like a pin,
A little sharp scratch.

It didn't really hurt, not much.
Rolling down my sleeve
I went back to our class.
And I was going to sit by Steve,
But there was Maggy in her place,
And to my great surprise
She had tears in her eyes.
'It wasn't as bad as that,'
I said. She burst out crying.
Crying! At her table! In Year Four!

I gave her a gum and sat by her.
Her face was on fire.
'It wasn't really bad,' she said.
'I was just frightened.' And Miss Lyon
Came over. 'Oh I'll leave her with you.
You're doing so well.' So I sat
By Maggy and we had a chat,
Not much – about this and that.
And that day a silence was broken.
Because I'd never ever spoken
        To Maggy before.

## Air Raids 1942

And waking in the night I used to hear
The trains at King's Cross, shunting in the dark,
The clash and clank of buffers, clear as clear,
And, carried on the black night air, the rush of steam,
While everybody slept. No raid tonight.

And perhaps some boy in Hamburg woke as well,
And heard his father in a neighbouring room
Quietly talking on, or radio static.
In London I heard footsteps sometimes in the street.
Perhaps he heard some too. Or aeroplanes.

## In Hospital

My tongue is mute.
The words are locked
Inside my head.
Beside my bed
A bowl of fruit,
And you who smile
And talk to me
And hold my hand,
I knew you in
Another time.
I know you still
But cannot speak.
My tongue is dead.
The words are shut
Inside my head.

## April

April Thackeray
The music teacher's daughter
Had eyes like skies
And hands like water.
She wore a shirt
Of daffodil yellow,
And we played duets
On her Pa's piano.

We never went out.
The simple fact is,
We only met
To play or practise,
And though I imagined
Walking beside her,
The gap between us
Could not have been wider.

April Thackeray
Was nobody's fool.
We shared the wide
Piano stool:
'One … and … two',
She'd lead, I'd follow,
When we played together
On her Pa's piano.

## February 5th 1940

*H*edges were huge and hostile,
Mist was clammy cold;
Dreading the village school
I trudged along. The war
Was in its early months
And I was eight years old;
I'd never, ever walked
A country lane before.

The school had naked walls
From which an oil-lamp hung.
Our hair was raked for nits
With sharp and scratchy combs;
And at our desks that day
We wore our coats, and sang,
'Somewhere Over the Rainbow',
Thinking of our homes.

## The Day My Father Died

The day my father died
A huge dark cloud
Rolled slowly over Berkeley Hill.
My uncles walked across the fields
From Rudcombe. I see them still,
In their dark, tight suits,
Their heavy feet dragging in the clay,
Three large men, in line abreast,
Outlined against the green.
And suddenly
The swirling rise
Of a flock of starlings
Against the sky's pewter grey.

## Boy on a Bike

When I pedal like mad along the lanes
  Or take a hill at dizzying speed,
I am not a boy on a bike, but a bird
  Flying, or a cloud scudding. Freed
For a while from the weight of the earth, I fly –
  And feel the air whizz past my face
And flap my shirt about my ribs.
  It's an incredible feeling! the power of pace!

But oh, the hills! The climbing. The pressing
  Downward to rise. The effort. The thick ache
In the legs, as I stand shoving the pedals,
  Zagging from side to side. Determined to make
The top. Failing. And dismounting. Heavily
  Wheeling the machine. Not a bird, just a lad.
Till at last I reach the highest point
  And again race down. Freewheeling. Shouting like mad!

## Yum!

*I* like pepper on my ice cream;
  Some like ice cream chilly.
I put ice cubes in the tea pot;
  Boiling tea is silly.

If you want your bread to harden,
  (Hard enough to chew)
Mix the flour with best cement
  And butter it with glue.

Some folks think this poem's stupid;
  Others think they're wrong.
Set it to a little tune
  And sing it as a song.

## Limerick Limerick

*T*here once was a poet of Limerick
And all his friends called him Eric
      His poems didn't scan
      Though he tried the best he can
      (I tried putting 'could'
      But it didn't sound as good),
And any way his name was really Derek.
And, what's more, neither Derek nor Eric rhymes with limerick.

## Stone

*A* firm fistful, earth-coloured,
This dull stone weights my arm –

Savage men on the uplands,
Pounders of skulls and grain –

With one hand I hold history,
Write with the other.

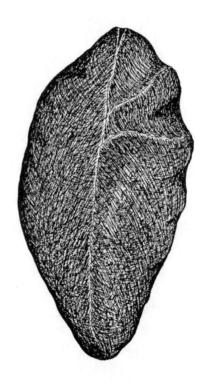

## Earth Apples

*W*hen I read in my old book
That in this island, long ago,
They ate cucumbers,
Calling them earth-apples,
I don't know why,
But my heart jumped for joy.

Now with my summer meals
I eat apples of the earth
In cool round slices,
And share the Garden of Eden
With a poet who lived
One thousand years ago.

*Gorse*

Gorse is a trumpet song.
    It spikes out of the earth,
        A welcome pain.

It will spear your hands.
    It will wound your skin,
        Bead you with scarlet.

It is 'I am' in all seasons.
    It blares its trumpet song
        *Tan-ta-ra* to the skies.

It is a still fire.
    Yellow on the hillsides,
        Coldly burning.

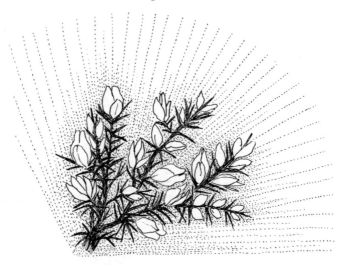

*i.m. Patricia O'Brien*

*M*y cousin died
In New End Hospital
One starry night in June.
That very day
I'd been to visit her –
Against the rule
No Children in the Ward –
But matron let me stay.

My hump-backed Patsy,
Propped between two pillows,
Her skin like tracing paper,
Spoke with pain,
Sent each word
On its separate voyage.
Like moths her blue hands
Fluttered on the counterpane.

I'd no idea
Of what to say to her
There in the Women's Ward
But stood and saw
How easily a person
Shrinks to nothing;
Patsy, so little left
Of what she'd been before.

## Matthew

Bent and old as he is, Matthew Harbour
  Knows a thing or two,
And for the price of a leisurely talk
  He'll tell them to you.

'I have lived in this one house all my life,
  And since I first begun,'
He says, 'water's run under that there bridge,
  Bubbling on and on.'

'Never be people again,' he says, 'who've seen
  The changes I've seen. Born
Before there were cars; now they orbits the stars.
  They call it a New Dawn.'

His face creases like a crumpling page
  As he winks at you.
'So long as I've been alive,' he says,
  'Every dawn was new.'

## After the Book is Closed

Whether it is the words
    or their meanings,
Or the sounds they make,
    or the way they echo one another;
Or simply the pictures
    they paint in the imagination
Or the ideas they begin,
    or their rhythms …

Whether it's the words
    or their histories,
Their curious journeys
    from one language to the next;
Or simply the shapes they make
    in the mouth –
Tongue and lips moving,
    breath flowing …

Whether it's the words
    or the letters used
To spell them, the patterns
    they make on the page;
Or simply the way they call feelings
    into the open
Like a fox seen suddenly in a field
    from a hurrying train …

Whether it's the words
        or the spaces between –
The white silences
        among the dark print,
I do not know.
        But I know this: that a poem
Will sing in my mind
        long after the book is closed.

## Yes But Sometimes

Yes. But sometimes I wake in the night,
For a long time, it seems.
And everyone in the house is asleep
And I can't get rid of my dreams.

And the curtains are not quite still,
And lights slide across the ceiling,
And I hear the voice of my own heart.
It's a peculiar feeling.

My thoughts get more and more muddled
And I feel as if I'm falling, falling
Into the dark. And I suppose I sleep;
Because next thing I hear Mum calling.

**Previous publication for poems in** *To Catch an Elephant*

Many of these poems previously appeared in *The Magnificent Callisto* and *Evidence of Elephants*. These are marked MC and EoE respectively; any previous 'first publication' is noted.

Two of the poems were among a sequence commissioned by the pianist David Howells, to accompany performances of *Prole do Bebe No 2,* by Villa-Lobos. Subtitled 'The Little Animals', it consisted of nine piano pieces. The poems were first performed in a recital at The Purcell Room, South Bank, and first published in *In Wordsworth's Chair.* These will be marked PdB.

| | |
|---|---|
| 'To Catch an Elephant' | EoE |
| 'A Small Star' | EoE |
| 'A Tale of Two Citizens' | EoE (and in *Does W Trouble You?*) |
| 'Oleg Popov the Clown' | EoE (and in *Strolling Players,* ed. Zenka and Ian Woodward, Evans 1978) |
| 'River Song' | EoE |
| 'Wasp' | MC |
| 'The Paper Beetle' | PdB |
| 'The Scholar's Cat' | EoE (and in *The Love of Cats* ed. Celia Haddon, Headline 1992) |
| 'The White Mouse' | MC |
| 'The Dragon and the Author' | MC (and in *TLS*) |
| 'The Dragon Speaks' | MC (and in *The Spectator*) |
| 'Three Birds' | MC |
| 'The Cat and the Pig' | MC |
| 'Ant Number 1,049,652' | MC |
| 'Evidence of Elephants' | EoE |
| 'Bei-shung' | EoE (and in *Headlines from the Jungle* ed. Anne Harvey & Virginia McKenna, Viking 1990) |
| 'The Cloth Bird' | PdB |
| 'Duffy' | MC |
| 'Fishing' | EoE |
| 'Spot the Difference' | EoE |
| 'Goal!' | EoE (and in *'Ere We Go* ed. David Orme, Piper Pan Macmillan Children's Books 1993) |
| 'Sir Bert' | EoE |
| 'Hlep!' | MC |

# Index of first lines